RANDOLPH CALDECOTT

The Man Who Could Not Stop Drawing

RANDOLPH CALDECOTT

The Man Who Could Not Stop Drawing

Leonard S. Marcus

FRANCES FOSTER BOOKS

Farrar Straus Giroux
New York

For my son, Jacob, *a doodler like his dad*

Farrar Straus Giroux Books for Young Readers
175 Fifth Avenue, New York 10010

Text copyright © 2013 by Leonard S. Marcus
All rights reserved
Color separations by Bright Arts (H.K.) Ltd.
Printed in China by South China Printing Co. Ltd., Dongguan City, Guangdong Province
Designed by Roberta Pressel
First edition, 2013
1 3 5 7 9 10 8 6 4 2

mackids.com

Library of Congress Cataloging-in-Publication Data
Marcus, Leonard S., 1950–
    Randolph Caldecott : the man who could not stop drawing / Leonard S.
Marcus. — First edition.
        pages cm
    ISBN 978-0-374-31025-7 (hardcover)
    1. Caldecott, Randolph, 1846–1886—Juvenile literature.
    2. Illustrators—England—Biography—Juvenile literature.   I. Title.
    NC978.5.C3M37 2013
    741.6'42092—dc23
    [B]
                                                                    2012050406

All images are by Randolph Caldecott unless otherwise noted.
We are grateful for permission to reprint the following images: Caldecott self-portrait on page 5: MS Typ 690.9, Houghton Library, Harvard University. Image on page 16: bMS Typ 690.1, Sketchbook S1, Houghton Library, Harvard University. Turner painting on page 18: © National Gallery / Art Resource, NY. Whistler painting on page 25: © Art Institute of Chicago Images. Images on page 27: bMS Typ 690.1, Sketchbook S3, Houghton Library, Harvard University. Image on page 34: The Kerlan Collection, University of Minnesota. Images on page 38 (bottom), page 45 (top), and page 49: © The Trustees of the British Museum. Images on pages 39 and 40: Whitworth Art Gallery, University of Manchester. Greenaway illustration on page 48: Eric Carle Museum of Picture Book Art. Bas relief on page 52: courtesy of Morton Schindel; photograph by Rob Zuckerman. Images on page 55 (bottom) and page 59: V & A Images / Victoria & Albert Museum.

Farrar Straus Giroux Books for Young Readers may be purchased for business or promotional use. For information on bulk purchases please contact Macmillan Corporate and Premium Sales Department at (800) 221-7945 x5442 or by email at specialmarkets@macmillan.com.

Self-portrait (undated)

wo swans at the water's edge trade bewildered glances when they notice a little frog poking his head out of the river. The frog is clutching a paper—a letter it would seem—which he reads with a look of total absorption.

The artist who sketched this delightful scene arranged matters so that the date on the frog's paper—13 Dec 1874—would be clearly visible to the young child receiving the picture in the mail. It was Christmastime, and this was Randolph Caldecott's response to a holiday gift containing a six-year-old's "grand sheet of drawings." In his accompanying message, Caldecott thanked the young artist, then added these words of encouragement: "I hope you will go on trying and learning to draw. There are many beautiful things waiting to be drawn. Animals and flowers oh! such a many—and a few people." It was a good wish for a talented six-year-old and one that Caldecott himself might have been glad for as a boy making his own first pictures.

RANDOLPH CALDECOTT was born, the third of John and Mary Caldecott's seven children, on March 22, 1846, in Chester, England, a walled fortress town built by the Romans around A.D. 70. Little is known about his parents or his early family life. The census of 1851 lists John, age thirty-eight, as a "retail hatter," but other records refer to him as an "accountant of standing." In all likelihood he was both. The Caldecotts lived in rooms on two floors above John's shop, together with two house servants and an apprentice who helped with the hat business.

Illness visited the Caldecotts often, although probably no more often than it did any of their neighbors. A son named William died at age two, only months after Randolph was born. The family's second daughter, Elizabeth, survived just six weeks during his third year. Then the children's mother, Mary Dinah Caldecott, died when Randolph was six. That same year he began to draw and to make animal figures out of wood and clay. As a boy, Caldecott himself suffered from rheumatic fever, a disease that permanently damaged his heart. Even so, he loved sports and exploring the outdoors, and rarely let his frail health stand in the way of a good time.

Watergate Street, Chester (artist unknown, 1850). The Caldecotts lived on nearby Bridge Street, which looked much like this.

A small building attached to Chester Cathedral housed the King's School, which Caldecott attended as one of fewer than twenty students. A single teacher, a Mr. James

Chester Cathedral (G. Prichard, 1850)

Harris, taught all the lessons, which included the study of English grammar and the classical Roman poets read in the original Latin. Caldecott received high marks despite not being "studious in the popular sense of the word" and preferring instead to spend "most of his leisure time in wandering in the country round," a friend later recalled. One of his old boyhood schoolbooks shows that Caldecott sometimes let his mind wander while in class: the future artist had freely doodled in the margins.

Tall, lanky, and good-looking, with blue-gray eyes and light brown hair that occasionally stood on end, he had a ready smile and easygoing manner and enjoyed poking fun at himself. His schoolmates chose him as their Head Boy, an honor roughly equivalent to student body president. He completed his formal education at fourteen, the usual age for boys given any schooling in a time when education was considered a luxury. Then, in 1861, with some prodding from his practical-minded father, he accepted a job as a clerk at the Whitchurch and Ellesmere Bank, in the nearby market town of Whitchurch, Shropshire. That year, Caldecott turned fifteen.

A bank clerkship was a highly desirable introduction to the world of work. It was a hard job to come by—John Caldecott most likely had to pay the bank something in return for hiring his son. The job paid well and held great promise for the future. In making these arrangements, Caldecott's father doubtless wished to provide his physically fragile son with a steady, dependable means of support.

Whatever his own thoughts about this, young Randolph made the best of his situation, taking up lodging with a farm couple two miles from town and making friends with his fellow clerks. For transportation, he had a dogcart—a lightweight horse-drawn vehicle—which he raced to town and back each day and made further use of for occasional business calls at the homes of the bank's far-flung customers. To his pleasure, he soon realized that the workload of a Whitchurch bank clerk left him with plenty of "off-time" for hunting, fishing, riding, hiking—and drawing. When Caldecott went for a walk down a country lane, he took along his sketchbook. During office hours, bank stationery did just as well.

Two pages from an undated, unpublished sketchbook, above and opposite page top

Drawing, for him, had already become much more than a pastime or even a serious hobby. Art, he had decided, was going to be his ticket out of the bank. Caldecott had no illusions that the sketches he was then making—humorous (but slight) pictures of people and realistic (but unremarkable) drawings of farm animals and landscapes—would earn him a living, let alone end up on the walls of a museum. But he knew that a person who drew well could hope to sell his sketches to the illustrated newspapers, more and more of which were setting up shop all around England just then. In 1855 alone, an astounding 168 new papers had appeared for sale at English newsstands and book stalls. With the coming of the railways, the English public had developed an insatiable appetite for news of the world—and the more pictures the better.

Caldecott wasted no time getting a toe in the door. Less than a year after arriving in Whitchurch, he sold his first drawing to a newspaper—in fact, the most popular of all of England's papers, the weekly *Illustrated London News*. He would have had to scramble every step of the way. The picture in question was an eyewitness sketch of the spectacular fire that all but destroyed the Queen's Railway Hotel in his hometown of Chester. Caldecott must have heard news of the blaze and dashed to the scene in his dogcart. He then would have had to make a finished drawing, pack it up for the editors of the *Illustrated London News*, and put the parcel on a train bound for London, where an engraving, based on the drawing, would be rapidly prepared by skilled artisans. The illustration ran in the paper's December 7, 1861, issue, a few days after the event it depicted. Caldecott was nowhere credited by name; still, more than 200,000 readers throughout Britain had seen an image based on his work.

Queen's Railway Hotel in flames (1861)

Scenes of Whitchurch from *The Great Panjandrum Himself* (1885), above,
and *An Elegy on the Death of a Mad Dog* (1879), below

Whitchurch, a thriving market town on the England-Wales border,
was a pleasant place to live. Had Caldecott wanted the quiet, carefree
life his father envisioned for him, he could have been very happy there
indeed. He must have known this himself. Years later, when he drew
the picture books for which he became famous, he showed his special
fondness for Whitchurch by recalling bits and pieces of the town in
his drawings: the tower of the Whitchurch Parish Church, the shops
along High Street, and an inn called The Swan all make appearances.

But Caldecott knew that only in a big city would he meet the art instructors who could help him perfect his craft and the editors and gallery owners who could launch his career. The nearest such city was Manchester, about forty miles to the northeast, and on Christmas Eve 1866 he applied for a clerkship at the offices of the Manchester and Salford Bank. He began work there the following March.

Manchester lacked the gilded pedigree, pomp, and splendor of London, but it had a swagger all its own. The epicenter of England's burgeoning textile industry, Manchester was a new kind of city. Its most imposing buildings, in the heart of town, were not the palaces of kings and queens but rather the fortress-like office blocks of newly rich mill owners, manufacturers, and bankers. The city had rapidly grown from a sleepy backwater town into an industrial-age colossus, and its steam-driven looms churned out mile after mile of affordable cotton cloth for sale and distribution throughout the world.

As Manchester's cotton mills multiplied, money poured into the city and its banks. People were hard-pressed to find words dramatic enough to describe the place and what was happening there. "Cottonopolis" became Manchester's nickname, always spoken with a mixture of pride and astonishment. "Manchester goods" became a new universal term for cotton cloth.

Not everyone in Manchester prospered, however, and much of the city's new growth was a sprawling expanse of grim, unsanitary, slapdash construction, a confusion of cavernous, smoke-billowing mill houses and the cramped slums where the mill workers lived. Working conditions in the mills were harsh and at times exceedingly dangerous, with the thick clouds of cotton dust that permeated the over-heated mills capable of damaging workers' lungs and eyes, and the machinery itself not only loud enough to cause deafness but also powerful enough to result in lost limbs and even fatalities. Still, people by the thousands from towns and villages throughout England and Ireland streamed into Manchester in search of higher-paying jobs at the mills.

A bird's-eye view of industrial Manchester (artist unknown, 1876)

Working-class Manchester girl, from an
undated, unpublished sketchbook

Child labor was deplorably widespread, with a substantial portion of those who worked in the mills—by one estimate approximately one in ten—under the age of thirteen. A series of reform laws enacted by Parliament, starting with the Cotton Factories Regulation Act of 1819, progressively raised the minimum age and shortened the maximum allowable workday for young people. Nonetheless, a great divide persisted throughout the nineteenth century in Britain between those children and teens who worked for a living and those with the unencumbered leisure to study and play.

Rich or poor, Caldecott and his contemporaries were all acutely aware of having been born into a remarkable age, an era of breathtaking changes in the way people worked, traveled, communicated, experienced time and space, and imagined the world. What was more, nearly all these changes were man-made—brought about by human ingenuity and the invention of new machines. Without these changes, Caldecott could not have had the career in art that he did.

Perhaps the most important of the new inventions was the steam engine, because it was the machine that powered so many other machines. Steam engines drove the locomotives that moved railway passengers and freight (including the illustrated magazines for which Caldecott had begun to work) at once-unimaginable speeds. For the first time ever, the new steam-powered passenger trains allowed travelers to traverse hundreds of miles in a single day. In 1846, the year Caldecott was born, England had just over two thousand miles of train track in service. By the time he was living in Manchester, the rail network had more than quintupled to nearly twelve thousand miles of track. In the next few years, Britain's mighty rail web would extend its reach into every nook and cranny of the nation.

Steam engines also powered the presses that printed the newspapers and magazines that gave illustrators like Caldecott a national audience, and which allowed millions of Englishmen and women to share, as never before, in a common awareness not only of current events but also of new books, manufactured goods, and places to visit. Steam engines powered the textile mills and other factories that had made England the richest nation on earth, and they were greatly increasing the wealth of other nations with access to the same technologies, including the United States. The textile mills of Manchester, New Hampshire, were closely modeled on those of Manchester, England. A new term—horsepower—entered the language as a measure of the power generated by these new engines, which in so many ways had made real horses a relic of an earlier age.

Artists could not help but respond to the great changes happening all around them, and trains, train stations, and the people who frequented them provided new subjects. Monumental paintings, called panoramas, became popular entertainments that people paid money to see. Seated in a theater, the audience watched wide-eyed as the panorama scrolled before them across the stage, a section at a time,

Manchester comic sketch (c. 1869)

creating the illusion of a journey through an unfamiliar and often exotic landscape. One of England's most original painters, Joseph Turner, produced an extraordinary, albeit much smaller, landscape titled *Rain, Steam, Speed*. Depicting a train in motion as little more than a blur of color in a radiant field of light, he succeeded in expressing what so many of his contemporaries felt: the story of the new age was above all a story about energy, swiftness, and motion.

Rain, Steam, Speed—The Great Western Railway, a painting by Joseph Mallord William Turner (1844)

Life in Manchester was faster paced by far than any that Caldecott had yet known. He started his new job on March 26, 1867. Late that night, having not yet unpacked his books, he wrote a letter to one of his closest Whitchurch friends, John Numerley. He included a quick sketch of himself standing forlornly by the fireplace in his new quarters, looking very much like someone who wished to be elsewhere. That first day, he reported, had come as a great jolt to him. Unlike in Whitchurch, employees of the Manchester and Salford Bank seemed to do nothing *but* work. The day commenced promptly at 9 a.m., by which time the clerks were expected to be at their desks as the first silk-hatted gentlemen customers strode into the banking hall. He teased his old friend that the shock of his new life had made him a believer in "predestination"—by which he meant the belief that everyone was born to live in some very particular, predetermined way. Caldecott was certain, he said, that it was God's wish that he should never work another day in his life. Alas, he noted, he was not likely to live out *that* destiny—not then or any time soon.

Caldecott settled into his demanding, new routine like the good sport he was. In later years he played down his prowess as a "quill-driver." But the bank's records show that the directors considered him a capable worker, and that they rewarded his labors accordingly with a series of raises. Even so, Caldecott managed to sneak in a bit of doodling on bank time—much to the delight of his best friend among his fellow clerks, William Clough, who got into the habit of saving the drawings. Eventually Clough made an album of them, which is now in the collection of London's Victoria and Albert Museum.

With a few rapid strokes of his pen, Caldecott would catch the look of a self-important customer, the amusing spectacle of a fellow clerk dozing off half-buried in a ledger, or, from memory, the swashbuckling swordfight seen in a play or the profile of a mule. William Clough would later say of Caldecott: "He came like a ray of sunlight into our life, and brightened the drudgery of our toil with his cheerful humour, and the

One of the first Caldecott illustrations published in *London Society* (1871)

Sketches of fellow bankers, from an undated,
unpublished Manchester sketchbook

playful sketches so easily done . . . So fertile was his invention, that a
chance blot on a piece of paper became in his hands the nucleus of a
happy drawing."

Even allowing for these occasional hijinks, Caldecott in Manchester must have felt that he led a double life. As a bank clerk, he labored six long days a week, with only Sundays off. After work on some evenings, he doubtless headed off with Clough and their comrades to a nearby pub for rounds of drinks. But on many nights Caldecott traded his bank ledger for a sketchbook and took to the streets, wandering the dimly lit byways of Manchester to draw the people and places he chanced upon. His younger brother Alfred recalled: "He made hundreds and thousands of disciplinary sketches at that time. The easy certainty with which, in maturity, he drew . . . was acquired [then]." Lost in concentration, Caldecott might forget about the hour and stay out drawing all night.

In Manchester he discovered other ways to advance his art career as well. The city had its share of artists, writers, and patrons of the arts, and of places where such people gathered. A short distance from the bank, the Royal Manchester Institution offered drawing lessons, public lectures on the arts and sciences, and an annual fall exhibition of paintings by local artists. At the Manchester School of Art, which had begun as a training center for textile designers, Caldecott took evening classes in painting. He also joined a new social club that recruited its members from the ranks of the city's poets, painters, journalists, actors, scientists, and other "gentlemen" with an interest in new ideas. At the Brasenose Club, Caldecott met all the editors who were in a position to hire him as an illustrator. Before long, his drawings were appearing regularly in two Manchester magazines, the *Will o' the Wisp* and *The Sphinx*. In 1869, he had a painting selected for the fall show at the Royal Manchester Institution.

More and more, Caldecott felt at home among people in the arts. An actor friend landed him a part as an extra in a play at the Manchester Theatre Royal. All Caldecott had to do was stand in a crowd, wave his arms wildly, and pretend to be cheering on the participants in a bicycle race. He found that he loved stepping out in front of an audience. Afterward, feigning heartbreak at not having come away a star from the experience, he wrote John Numerley, "I was not [even] mentioned in the papers as a promising actor."

He also joined the city Glee Club. Caldecott sang bass, and once again he could not resist making fun of himself. Writing to John Numerley, he claimed to become so completely absorbed in his singing that he routinely strayed from the music as written and also

Caldecott, center right, bent over, was a lot more graceful than he made himself out to be in his amusing sketch of a Manchester fancy-dress ball (c. 1869).

forgot that he was not the evening's soloist. "I am so packed with feeling," he confided tongue in cheek, "that I am perpetually tapped on the shoulder, pinched on the leg, or stabbed with a tuning-fork, and asked if I think that mine is the principal part . . . By a few years' training it is expected that my voice might become somewhat musical."

Caldecott lived at three different addresses during his five years in Manchester. It was not by chance that with each move he put himself farther away from the bank. In May of 1870, he made a quick trip to London to test the waters for a change of careers. He went armed with a portfolio of drawings and with the hope of meeting some of the city's important editors, securing work from them, and returning home with a clear idea of what it would mean to quit his bank job and live in London.

A young artist presents his work to an editor in *London Society* (1871).

High on his list of people to see was Thomas Armstrong, a fellow Manchester man fourteen years his senior. Armstrong had long ago made the big leap that Caldecott was now contemplating. Once in London, the older man had not only succeeded brilliantly as a painter but had also become legendary as an art world power broker, a man whose opinions mattered to all the city's editors, gallery owners, and critics. He took an immediate liking to Caldecott.

"The Two Trombones," in *London Society* (1871)

Months passed before he got around to it, but by the fall of that year Armstrong had passed along some of Caldecott's drawings to the editor of a stylish monthly called *London Society*, with a letter urging him to give Caldecott an assignment. The editor, Henry Blackburn, did as he was advised. In the years that followed, he and Armstrong became Caldecott's two closest friends. The first of Caldecott's many illustrations for *London Society* appeared in the issue for February of 1871, and soon he was one of the magazine's regulars.

One of a series of hunting friezes for *London Society* (1871–72)

Cousin Honeycomb's Railway Alphabet (artist unknown, 1852), left, exemplifies the older, more static way of arranging words and images in a children's picture book. In contrast, *The Railroad Alphabet* (artist unknown, 1889), below, clearly shows the influence of Caldecott's livelier touch.

As his ties to London multiplied, Caldecott spent more and more time in the great city. "Manchester to London in 5 hrs," he noted with amazement in a sketchbook, recording the time it had taken to make the journey south by train. Covering the same distance by horse-drawn coach might consume twenty or more hours. Train travel also made the journey far smoother going—even enjoyable. The train traveler could sit back in upholstered comfort and read, or stand up and stretch his legs, or even go for a stroll as farmlands, country villages, and entire cities swept past with incredible speed. The view out the window seemed a kind of magic trick, and yet it was perfectly real.

Caldecott discovered another benefit of rail travel. The pulsing rhythm, like a steady drumbeat, of the great iron-wheel works pounding underfoot somehow inspired him to draw in the freest possible way. As he sat drawing in his passenger seat, his hand moved across the page as though in time with the driving speed of the train.

Caldecott was not the only man of imagination to have had this exhilarating experience. So too did Charles Dodgson, the Oxford mathematics professor, who famously composed nonsense tales and rhymes for children under the name Lewis Carroll. Dodgson was chugging along aboard a train

Illustration by John Tenniel from *Through the Looking-Glass* by Lewis Carroll (1871)

when the chapter titles for *Alice's Adventures in Wonderland* all came to him.

No longer a stranger in London, Caldecott was getting to know some of the most famous artists of his day. John Tenniel, the illustrator of Lewis Carroll's *Alice*, was also the head cartoonist for England's leading humor magazine, *Punch*. George du Maurier was *Punch*'s number two illustrator and perhaps England's finest line artist. The daring American painter James McNeill Whistler lived in London and always had some controversy swirling around him. Caldecott crossed paths with all these remarkable men, studied their work at close range, and saw how they lived.

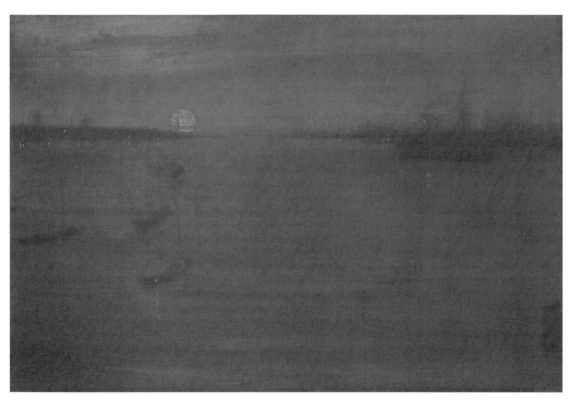

Nocturne: Blue and Gold—Southampton Water, a painting by James McNeill Whistler (1872). Whistler showed that less could indeed be more in art. Caldecott later applied this lesson in his spare but animated picture book drawings.

Turning his back on the security of his bank job took great cour-age. When Caldecott announced his intention to do so, one of the managers cautioned him, perhaps with affection, that the streets of London were not paved with gold. He was twenty-six when he moved to London at the start of 1872, with just enough money to last him a year. Caldecott rented two rooms on the top floor of the ivory-colored four-story building at 46 Great Russell Street, directly across from the British Museum.

46 Great Russell Street today

It was the perfect perch for an artist determined to hone his skills. As an illustrator, Caldecott knew he might be called upon to draw just about anything. If he wished to practice drawing the human figure, the British Museum had one of the world's great collections of classical

Greek and Roman sculpture. If he wanted to study animal anatomy, the museum had a comprehensive collection of animal skeletons and preserved specimens, from birds and insects to giraffes. The museum housed ancient manuscripts, rare books, art and artifacts from the Middle East and Asia, coins and armor from the European Middle Ages. It was all there for him, just inside the gates of the vast, encyclopedic museum. In his diary he reported spending an evening "making a drawing, and measuring [the] skeleton of a white stork." A week later he returned for an even closer look: "Had storks out of cases to examine insertion of wing feathers." Other days he stood in the broad expanse of the museum's courtyard and painted the pigeons.

Undated, unpublished sketchbooks, including
one set of drawings done at the "B[ritish] Museum"

If he wanted to sketch the high and mighty government men of the day—newspapers always needed pictures of this kind—he could walk to the Houses of Parliament in less than half an hour, sit in the public gallery, and sketch everyone from the Prime Minister on down. Or, if he strolled just as far in the opposite direction, he could take a seat in one of London's courts of law and record the proceedings there.

Three scenes from Parliament for the *Pictorial World* (1874). At top right, the gentleman rising to speak is Prime Minister Benjamin Disraeli.

Soon after his arrival in London, Caldecott enrolled in a life drawing class taught by one of England's most renowned painters, Edward Poynter. At the same time, he sought new ways to earn a living from his art. That June, he published his first drawing in *Punch* and, a few months later, made his debut in the elegant weekly newspaper *The Graphic*. Before the year was out, Caldecott had four of his drawings chosen for inclusion in a group show, the "Black-and-White" exhibition of graphic art presented in the Dudley Gallery of Egyptian Hall, a popular attraction in the heart of London.

Caldecott's first drawing in *Punch* (1872)

In a year of exciting advances, his greatest adventure began with an invitation from Henry Blackburn to accompany him to the Harz Mountains of northern Germany. Blackburn was writing a travel guide for English and American tourists about the rugged, tradition-soaked region that, thanks to the coming of the railways, foreign travelers were just discovering for themselves. Blackburn wanted Caldecott to illustrate the book.

That August, the Midlands country lad who had never before set foot beyond Britain's shores headed off to meet Blackburn and his wife in a foreign land and found that he loved to travel. He had packed a German phrase book and easily charmed the Germans he met with his awkward but good-natured attempts at speaking their language. All the while, he filled his sketchbook with the drawings he needed. The

An illustration from *The Harz Mountains* (1873)

book was published the following year with a quaint title meant to pique readers' curiosity and remind them of the fairy tales of their childhood: *The Harz Mountains: A Tour of the Toy Country*.

Blackburn must have been a fireball of energy. No sooner had he returned to London than he sold some of his friend's drawings to *The Graphic*. Then Blackburn was off once more, this time on a steamship bound for New York, where he showed the Harz Mountain drawings to the city's top editors. *Harper's New Monthly* chose twenty-two of Caldecott's illustrations to accompany an excerpt from Blackburn's book. The New York *Daily Graphic* took several, too, and asked Caldecott to be their "London artistic correspondent." Much to his surprise, Caldecott now had steady work for major publications on both sides of the Atlantic.

Cover image for *The Daily Graphic* (1873)

In his impressive new correspondent's role, Caldecott traveled to Vienna during the summer of 1873 to cover the World Exposition. Part temporary museum, part theme park and carnival sideshow, the Vienna exposition was the latest in a series of grand spectacles designed to highlight each of the participating nations' latest achievements in the arts and sciences. Among its stagier attractions were life-size re-creations of a Japanese temple and a section of the old city of Jerusalem.

Vienna fairgoers (1873)

Closer in spirit to the exposition's primary goal was an exhibit that combined innovation in art and science, presented by the English-born American photographer Eadweard Muybridge. The flamboyant artist/inventor who for a time wished to be known only as "Helios" (after the Greek sun god!) had lately immersed himself in photographic experiments aimed at solving an age-old riddle: whether or not there was ever a moment, as a horse ran at a gallop, when all four of its legs left the ground. Muybridge knew that the only way to find this out for sure would be to invent a new kind of camera that could capture much tinier slivers of time than any camera then in existence. With financial backing from the California railroad tycoon and racehorse owner

Photo sequence by Eadweard Muybridge for his *Animals in Motion* series begun in 1872

Leland Stanford, who had posed the challenge to him, Muybridge set to work on a project that in a matter of years would make his name known throughout the world.

Muybridge had come to Vienna with examples of a different side of his extraordinary body of work: his "mammouth" (as he called them) photographs of Yosemite National Park. These photographs depicted wilderness landscapes thought to have remained unchanged for thousands of years, places where, in a sense, time stood still. But Muybridge was equally drawn to facets of the natural world—waterfalls, for example—that were in a constant state of flux. Half-hidden amid the monumental rocks and trees of his epic landscape photographs, a ghostly whir of water—the image of a moment in time captured—would complicate the scene, leaving the viewer suddenly aware that change was everywhere, even in the stateliest, most ancient spots on earth.

Did Caldecott see Muybridge's photographs in Vienna? The Yosemite pictures won Muybridge a gold medal at the exposition, recognition that all but guaranteed that *The Daily Graphic*'s correspondent would have made a point of viewing them. Did Caldecott take an interest, as well, in Muybridge's most famous photographic experiments, those in which he attempted to stop time photographically in order to see, far more precisely than was possible with the naked eye, the continuously changing sequence of movements made by a galloping horse? Although we do not know for sure, it seems likely that he would have been utterly fascinated. The very best bits of evidence we have for thinking this are the illustrations of a galloping horse and rider in Caldecott's picture book *The Diverting History of John Gilpin*, including the one upon which the image depicted on the Caldecott Medal is based.

Line illustrations from *The Diverting History of John Gilpin* (1878), above and at bottom

The full-color illustration adapted for the image depicted on the Caldecott Medal

Back home in London that fall of 1873, Caldecott attended a lecture given by Mark Twain at the Queen's Concert Rooms. Counting on his English fans *not* to know him by sight, the American author had played a prank by stepping onstage in formal attire and addressing the crowd as though he were the theater manager with a last-minute cancellation to announce. Amid the rising groans of disappointed onlookers, he began by stating that Mr. Clemens had fully expected to be present. Then, raising a hand for silence, he cinched the joke by assuring the audience that fortunately Mark Twain *was* present, and would now proceed to deliver his lecture. The audience roared its approval and settled in to hear Twain dissect the "savage" manners and customs of the inhabitants of the faraway Sandwich Islands—a way of life, he concluded, that was hardly distinguishable from that of the inhabitants of London and New York. Delighted, Caldecott wrote a friend that he had found the famously irreverent American "very hearable."

Caldecott was game to experiment with other types of art besides illustration: "Do you want a sign-board?" he wrote, only half in jest, to his Whitchurch friend William Etches, "or an equestrian statue? Or an elegant wallpaper? Anything in that line I shall be happy to attend to." Earlier that year, when Caldecott met a French sculptor living in London named Jules Dalou, he had told his new acquaintance that he wished to learn how to sculpt in clay. Dalou had replied that *he* wished to learn to speak good English. The two men agreed to trade lessons. Working in Dalou's studio, Caldecott produced several sculptures, including a wonderful one of a cat ready to pounce.

Crouching Cat, life-size terra-cotta sculpture (c. 1874)

As Caldecott became better known, more people approached him with projects of one kind or another. At the start of 1874, it was a new book to illustrate, a collection of short stories by the first American literary writer to achieve fame both in England and at home, Washington Irving. Caldecott agreed to make more than one hundred drawings for *Old Christmas: From the Sketch Book of Washington Irving*, which included such classic tales as "Rip Van Winkle" and "The Legend of Sleepy Hollow."

Illustrations, above and below, from *Old Christmas* (1875)

Illustrating Irving's book was the most ambitious challenge Caldecott had undertaken so far. As he labored day after day in a wooden shed in the garden of a friend's country house, sketching pictures of hunting dogs, stagecoach drivers, and country houses in snow-covered fields, he began to question his ability to do justice to the great writer's stories. He had, after all, only had a smattering of formal art training, and he had never visited America, where the writer's best-known stories were set. The big job was weighing heavily on him. "I have now got a workshop," he wrote a friend, "and I sometimes wish that I was a workman." When January of 1875 rolled around, Caldecott was still fretting about all the ways in which he had not yet become the artist and person he wished to be. Among his New Year's resolutions that January was: "Only . . . talk of matters about which there [is] a reasonable probability that I [know] something."

That fall, *Old Christmas* appeared in bookshops

Illustration from *Old Christmas* (1875)

in time for the holidays. It sold well in both England and America. The drawings that Caldecott had so worried over were the best he had ever done, and critics had nothing but praise. "The world," Henry Blackburn wrote afterward of this turning point in his friend's career, had "discovered a new genius." When he least expected it, Randolph Caldecott had made his name.

Perhaps the best lesson Caldecott learned from that terrible time of self-doubt was not to spread himself too thin. When a friend told him of a potential client who was eager to have him paint a series of landscapes to order—scenes, most likely, of the countryside around the gentleman's home—Caldecott said no. Other artists, he suggested, could do a better job of it. In any case, landscapes were not really in his "line." What *did* he consider to be his specialty? "Please say that my line is to make to smile the lunatic who has shown no sign of mirth for many months." Aware that his sense of humor could get the better of him, Caldecott also turned down requests for portraits, concerned that his talent for caricature might result in a likeness that made his subject look too ridiculous. "I fear," he confided to a friend, "that I ought not to approach Mrs Green brush in hand—my brush is not a very reverent one."

The great success of *Old Christmas* spurred demand for a second Irving story collection. Once again, Caldecott rose to the challenge, this time a lot more confidently. *Bracebridge Hall* appeared in the fall of 1877. From then onward, he always had at least one book project in the works, and with the constant call for his drawings in newspapers and magazines, Caldecott had little time for rest.

Illustration from *Bracebridge Hall* (1877)

While the popular notion of the artist was that of an unfettered and carefree spirit, Caldecott now found himself working every bit as hard as he had at the bank. "I stick pretty close to business," he wrote one of his Manchester friends, "pretty much in that admirable and attentive manner which was the delight, the pride, the exaltation of the great chiefs who strode . . . through the Manchester banking halls." He was hardly complaining; far from it. Still, it must have amused Caldecott to see in himself even a hint of the stern taskmasters who had lorded it over him during his quill-driving days. The Manchester and Salford Bank had prepared him for his new life in ways he would never have thought possible.

When time permitted, Caldecott headed for the countryside to roam to his heart's content, pausing to draw whatever caught his eye. In a letter sent on a beautiful spring day from near Whitchurch, where he was enjoying a leisurely visit with friends, Caldecott wrote slyly: "I feel I owe somebody an apology for staying in the country so long, but don't quite see to whom it is due, so I shall stay two or three days longer."

Graphite drawing from an undated, unpublished sketchbook, top, and watercolor study, above

Early in 1878, a white-bearded gentleman came to see Caldecott in his rooms at 46 Great Russell Street to talk over a business proposition. Edmund Evans, a printer famous throughout England for his skill at producing illustrated books in color, was an admirer of Caldecott's drawings for *Old Christmas* and *Bracebridge Hall*. As Caldecott well knew, he was also the enterprising man responsible for engaging his friend and professional rival, Walter Crane, as the illustrator of a long-running popular series of Sixpenny Toybooks, or children's picture books.

Self-portrait by Walter Crane (1883)

Crane illustrated the first of his books for Evans in 1865. Thirteen years later, he had grown tired of doing them and, with no end of other projects to keep him occupied, told Evans he wished to retire from the field. Evans had come to Caldecott hoping to persuade him to take over for Crane.

While some printers did their work on the cheap, in the quickest, easiest possible way, Evans preferred to take his time and aim for a result that he and his illustrators would all be proud of. He favored subtle colors over the more garish, circus-y ones. He thought of the illustration, design, and printing of children's books as an art. All this was very much to Caldecott's liking, as was the chance to illustrate a different kind of book. The artistic reporter's frantic life of rushing from one news event to the next had taken its toll, and the prospect of immersing himself in a long-term series held great appeal. Still, there were other questions to consider, including what Caldecott would be paid.

Walter Crane, who lacked a head for business, had accepted a modest one-time payment for each of the books he created for Evans. As a result, no matter how many copies of the books sold, Crane never received another penny for his labors on top of the initial fee. Caldecott was quite plain about his unwillingness to agree to the same terms, and proposed instead to place a kind of wager on the success of his toybooks. If not a single copy of the books sold, Caldecott told Evans that he would take absolutely nothing for his services. But for every copy that *did* sell, he would be entitled to a small portion of the one-shilling price. If the books proved to be a grand success, the royalties would add up, year after year, perhaps for the rest of his life.

The two men also talked about the look and design of the books Caldecott might do. Caldecott had studied Walter Crane's picture books and had serious reservations about them. Crane's illustrations, he thought, were too stiff and fussy, with every square inch of the picture frame packed with detail. Crane may have felt that he was giving more to his readers, and his illustrations *did* sometimes have a kind of treasure-chest appeal. More often, though, Caldecott found Crane's illustrations lifeless.

An illustration by Walter Crane from *Beauty and the Beast* (1874)

Evans assured Caldecott that he did not expect him to do anything remotely similar, and that the quality he liked best about Caldecott's drawings was their casualness and freedom, the impression they gave of having simply flowed from his pen onto the page. No other illustrator Evans worked with knew the secret of drawing in this way. Crane and any number of others could produce a drawing of a horse that looked precisely like a horse. But Caldecott alone knew how to make the horse *gallop*. Even more remarkably, he worked this magic with just a very few well-placed lines.

He and Evans agreed that each picture book would have a small number of formal color paintings and, interspersed among them, a larger number of rapid-fire line sketches, the latter printed in brown ink for the warmer feeling it conveyed compared with the standard black. Combining two types of artwork in a single book would present fascinating opportunities to experiment with layout and design. The final result, whatever it proved to be, was sure to look unlike any children's book that had come before it.

Illustration from *The Fox Jumps Over the Parson's Gate* (1883)

Still Caldecott hesitated, and it was not until he visited Evans at the printer's country house some weeks later that he finally said yes. It is not known who chose the subjects of the first two books in the series afterward known as R. Caldecott's Picture Books: the comic ballad about a shopkeeper

Illustrations from *The Diverting History of John Gilpin* (1878)

who rides a runaway horse called *The Diverting History of John Gilpin* and a favorite old Mother Goose rhyme, *The House That Jack Built*. When for the latter book it came time to draw the "cat that killed the rat / that ate the malt that lay in the house that Jack built," Caldecott remembered the sculpture of the crouching cat he had made in the London studio of Jules Dalou.

Illustrations from *The House That Jack Built* (1878), including "lightning sketches" for the book and an illustration of a cat based on Caldecott's own sculpture of a few years earlier (see page 34)

As Caldecott himself leaped headlong into the new project, he realized the freedom that was now his to put people and places he knew to good use in the drawings. In *The Babes in the Wood*, one of the two books he created the following year, he teased Evans by making him the model for one of the "ruffians strong." In a bittersweet nod to his always-shaky health, he cast himself as the light-haired, bearded man "sore sicke . . . and like to dye" who leaves behind the two children whose adventures form the core of the tale.

Illustrations from *The Babes in the Wood* (1879). Printer Edmund Evans is pictured, top, at far left.

Undated study of waders in Brittany

To many illustrators, producing two complete picture books in the space of a few months' time would be a daunting challenge, the more so for an artist new to the genre. But if Caldecott was worried, he showed no sign of it. That summer, he headed for the Brittany coast, in France, to rest and sun himself at a seaside hotel and to make sketches of his picturesque surroundings both for *The Graphic* and for the latest travel book he had agreed to illustrate.

Caldecott had his own affectionate name for Brittany: "the land of cider and sardines." He arrived determined to enjoy himself and to avoid having to wander high and low in search of subjects for his illustrations. His brilliant idea, as he wrote his friend William Clough, was in effect to let his subjects find him. One month into the job, however, he had to admit that he was feeling all but exhausted anyway. "Sitting on Inn benches, under pretence of studying and sketching the forms of the passersby . . . is somewhat unhinging to a mind dwelling in a body not over-robust."

Back in London, as he sat down to do the artwork for his first picture books, Caldecott considered the

Self-portrait drawn in Brittany (1878)

various options open to him. He could draw the standard kind of illustration, with the story's main characters positioned more or less at the center of the image, like actors onstage engaged in some action or other. Or he could give readers, in a quicker, more casual kind of sketch, a close-up view of a particular detail of the scene: the dog that "worried the cat" in *The House That Jack Built*; the table set for dinner in *John Gilpin*. These smaller line drawings might be placed *anywhere* on the page, as might the words of text that accompanied them. Some pages might even be left almost entirely blank, with just a single small drawing or a very few words to carry the story forward. Time might be made to pass—in a kind of flash-forward effect—between the action depicted in the drawing on the left-hand side of a page and that seen across from it on the right. Even the page-turn could be made dramatic, surprising readers with a sudden blast of color or (as he first did for the second set of books a year later, in *An Elegy on the Death of a Mad Dog*) establishing a rhythm

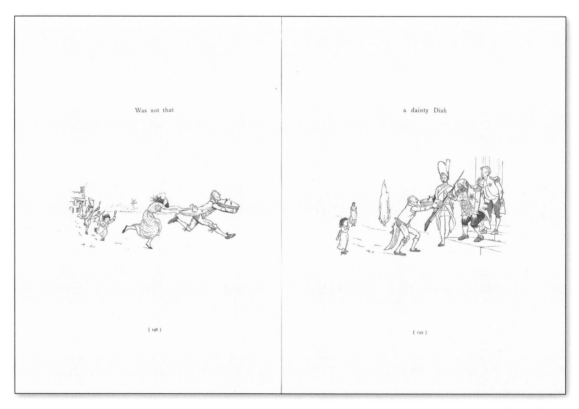

Time flashes forward from left to right in this page opening from *Sing a Song for Sixpence* (1880) . . .

by extending a single line of text over a number of pages, each with its picture, like a tantalizing secret revealed one small bit at a time.

Caldecott realized there was nothing stopping him from introducing characters and other story elements in his pictures that were nowhere mentioned in the text. The illustrations might tell a second story that somehow complemented the one told in words. Readers would have fun weaving the two story strands together.

. . . then moves from right to left (top image) and again from left to right (bottom image).

That fall, as Caldecott awaited publication of the first of his picture books, Edmund Evans invited both him and Kate Greenaway—another artist Evans had engaged to make children's books—to spend the weekend at his country house, forty miles southwest of London. Among Evans's Witley neighbors was the great English novelist George Eliot, who while chatting with Greenaway happened to mention a pair of twins who lived in a nearby village. It was decided that the illustrators should go have a look for themselves.

Gathering up their art supplies, they piled into a carriage and trotted off to be greeted by the twins' proud mother, who hoped of course that at least one of the artists would immortalize her children in the pages of a book. In a letter to William Clough, Caldecott told what

Illustration by Kate Greenaway from *Little Ann and Other Poems*, by Jane and Ann Taylor (1883).
Inset: photograph of Kate Greenaway (undated).

Undated comic drawing featuring a Kate Greenaway–designed girl's outfit. Caldecott, far right, scrambles to catch up with his fellow artists, including Greenaway herself.

happened next: "A history of the twins was kindly given by the mother, how they lived together, ate together, slept together, walked together, did everything together. Interesting. My opinion was that they were 2 fat, ugly children who looked as though they laid down to their food and slobbered it up."

Evans printed 10,000 copies each of *The House That Jack Built* and *The Diverting History of John Gilpin*. When both books sold out immediately, he put through an order for the second of several additional printings. As demand for the books continued to build, Caldecott closed out the year of 1878 by heading to the south of France for a much-needed rest. It was at his hotel in Cannes, hundreds of miles from home, that he had his first real taste of celebrity. During his stay, there appeared in the newspapers read by his fellow guests some wildly enthusiastic reviews of the new children's books by an illustrator named Randolph Caldecott. On learning that he, too, was named Caldecott, they begged to know if he was "any relation to the gifted artist."

English ladies and gents enjoy their holiday in warmer climes in this illustration for an article titled "Flirtations in France" in *The Graphic* (1879).

Caldecott had never imagined being asked such a question, but he had tried to anticipate how and where his books would be sold, and what might make them stand out for shoppers. In designing the covers, he had taken into account that the books would be featured at railway platform bookstalls all across England. With this in mind he set out to create cover designs bold enough to be "catching," as he told a friend, "from the top of an omnibus or out of the passing window of a railway carriage."

"Modern Advertising: A Railway Station in 1874," by Alfred Concanen (1874), depicts London's bustling Charing Cross Station. Caldecott's books were sold throughout England at W. H. Smith & Son stalls, like the one pictured here at lower right.

From 1878 onward, Caldecott completed two picture books a year for Evans. Early the following year, while on yet another European excursion (this time to Italy), he was already at work on the second pair. "I scribbled out the plan for 1 book in the train between Florence and Bologna," he wrote later that year to William Clough. He finished some of the art for *The Babes in the Wood* (or possibly *An Elegy on the Death of a Mad Dog*; he didn't say which) before returning to London.

Illustrations from *The Babes in the Wood* (1879), top, and *An Elegy on the Death of a Mad Dog* (1879), bottom. The title of the latter book appears in a catchier, shortened form on the front cover and is given in full on the title page.

"Feeding the Calves," hand-tinted terra-cotta bas-relief, undated

That fall of 1879, in the weeks before the second set of books appeared, Caldecott briefly took up sculpting again and made decorative carvings of birds for some of the interior columns of a special house under construction on the outskirts of London. It belonged to Frederic Leighton, a celebrated painter and president of England's Royal Academy. What made the house most remarkable was the extravagance of the plan for its main rooms, and in particular for the big open central space called Arab Hall. Situated on the ground floor, Leighton's pride and joy had a high domed ceiling, a reflecting pool,

lavish blue tile work, elaborate woodcarving, and touches of gold everywhere. It was all like a vision out of *The Arabian Nights*. Leighton built it as a gathering place for his legions of artist friends, a great many of whom had taken up residence around nearby Holland Park, as Caldecott himself would do.

Caldecott longed to be in the country, however, and that same fall he rented a modest house in the village of Kemsing,

twenty miles southeast of London. It is "an
out-of-way place," he told a friend, "but
exactly right for me." He had a garden, a
dogcart, a chestnut mare, and a "comical young dachshund" named Lalla-
Rookh, after the title character of an
English love poem set in exotic Persia.

It was also about then that Caldecott
himself fell in love. The following March, he
married Marian Brind, a London wine merchant's daughter four
years younger than him. "We were married at a small church in Kent,"
he wrote a friend afterward. "My best man drove me in a dog-cart. I
sold him my mare on the way." The couple spent their honeymoon in
Venice, where Caldecott found gondola travel very much to his liking:
"easy, smooth, and soul-subduing—especially by moonlight and when
the ear is filled with the rich notes of a very uncommon gondolier's
voice and the twanging of a sentimental traveller's lute." From then
onward, he and Marian were almost always together. In 1881, she was
his model for the title character of his picture book *The Queen of Hearts*.

Now when Caldecott went to London it was usually for a quick trip, perhaps just to make needed sketches of a particular model. He could afford to live wherever he wanted. In 1882, he took a twenty-one-year lease on a country house in Frensham, Surrey, where he kept a riding horse named Merry-legs, and, for his London sojourns, he purchased the brick row house at 24 Holland Street, a short walk from Leighton House and the homes of some of his other artist friends. Caldecott built a studio for himself in the garden behind his new residence, so that he could feel he was in the country even when he was not. Despite periodic bouts of illness and the constant pressures of work—"People," he wrote a friend, "for whom I promised to make drawings are so unreasonable as to ask me to fulfil my promises in a reasonable time"—he had never been happier.

Meanwhile, his picture books continued to grow in popularity and were becoming well known to children in America as well as in England. He kept the work interesting for himself by constantly experimenting with the art form and by continuing to make playful reference to people and places from his own life. In *Sing a Song for Sixpence*, he recalled his banking days in his drawing of the boy king sitting

The King's Counting-house wall sports paintings of Robinson Crusoe and Friday and the biblical David and Goliath.

"in his Counting-house, counting out his money." In his drawings for "Hey Diddle Diddle," one of the two Mother Goose rhymes he illustrated in 1882, he greatly enlarged upon the tiny kernel of a story hinted at in the text, depicting an animated chorus of comical barnyard creatures and suggesting what might possibly have happened to the dish and the spoon just *after* they ran away together.

In 1883, he drew his first (and only) book populated entirely by animals in human dress, *A Frog He Would A-Wooing Go*. By then, the picture books had become so widely admired that art collectors were prepared to pay good money for the original drawings. In 1884, a London gallery, acting on Caldecott's behalf, sold two illustrations from the frog book to a wealthy barrister named Rupert Potter. The collector's daughter, Beatrix, not only enjoyed the Caldecott originals that hung on the walls of the family's elegant South Kensington home but, determined to become an artist herself, she also studied them. In this way, Beatrix Potter, afterward the creator of Peter Rabbit, Jeremy Fisher, and other classic picture book characters in human dress, taught herself vital lessons about drawing.

The title character in *A Frog He Would A-Wooing Go* may have inspired Beatrix Potter's well-dressed frog hero Jeremy Fisher.

"On the Way Out—A big steamer like this never Rolls," an illustration drawn in rough seas on board the *Aurania* (1885), and published a year later in *The Graphic*

On October 31, 1885, Caldecott and his wife set off on their most adventurous journey together, boarding a steamship in Liverpool bound for New York City. As usual, he had two plans in mind for the trip: to rest and relax in the sunshine and warmth of some of the points on their itinerary, especially Florida and California; and to find distinctly American subjects to draw. On his return home, Caldecott intended to publish a sketchbook of his far-flung American travels.

He had not chosen an ordinary ship on which to make the arduous ten-day voyage. Just a year before, the Cunard Line's *Aurania* had beaten its two nearest rivals in an informal race to determine the world's fastest seagoing vessel. Travel on such a ship was apt to yield a scene or two worth recording by an illustrator, as well as to maximize the chances for a smooth and comfortable crossing. Or so Caldecott might well have thought.

The *Aurania* encountered rough seas that left Marian ill for much of the time and her husband, who was not all that strong to begin with, feeling light-headed and exhausted. They made landfall in New York on November 9 and then, despite the pummeling they had just endured, almost immediately boarded a train heading south. "We hope," Caldecott wrote a friend, the English poet Frederick Locker-

Lampson, from Philadelphia, the couple's first stop en route to St. Augustine, Florida, that "there will be an overland route discovered by the time of our return." From Philadelphia, they continued on to Washington, D.C., where Caldecott sketched the people in the Capitol Rotunda, then to Richmond, Charleston, Savannah, and St. Augustine. From there, the couple intended to travel west by train to Colorado and California, and then slowly make their way back to New York to explore America's most dynamic city at their leisure before heading home from Boston.

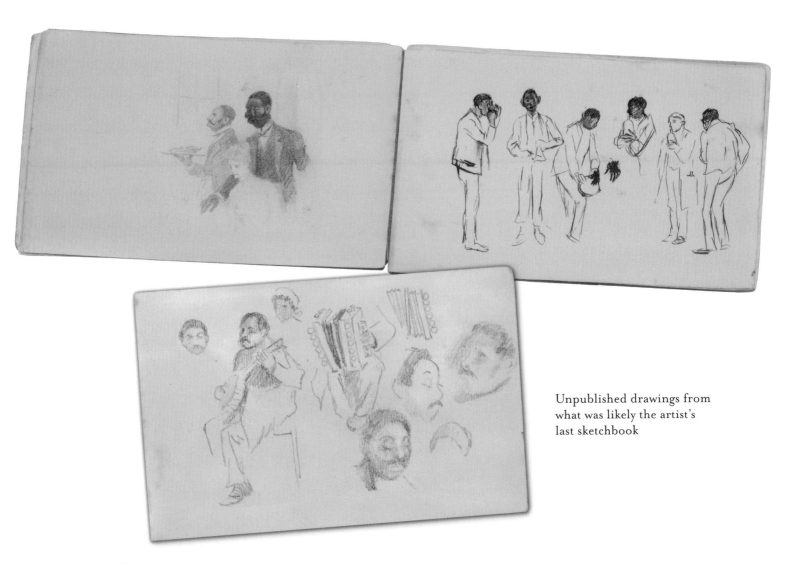

Unpublished drawings from what was likely the artist's last sketchbook

In Florida, however, things did not go as planned. The Caldecotts discovered that St. Augustine, which they reached in mid- or late December, would not be the sunny, restful place they had imagined. The entire state of Florida was caught in the grip of an historic cold spell. Feeling unwell when he arrived, Caldecott took to his bed.

A few weeks later, he seemed to rally. Then, however, his strength doubtless undermined by exposure to the chill air, Caldecott went into a steep decline. He developed an acute case of gastritis, a painful inflammation of the lining of his stomach that was nothing new to him. On February 13, 1886, a month short of his fortieth birthday, Randolph Caldecott died. The cause of death, according to the official report, was "organic disease of the heart." Following his burial in St. Augustine's Evergreen Cemetery, a deeply shaken Marian Caldecott returned home to England alone.

The Caldecotts had no children of their own, but the picture books the artist left behind have touched the lives of millions of young people. In addition, countless artists have turned to the books for inspiration—and for an understanding of how still pictures can be made to move across the page. At first glance, Caldecott's books might appear to be quaintly old-fashioned. (In one respect, they *were* old-fashioned even when new, as Caldecott typically set his stories in the tranquil, pre-industrial towns and villages of Georgian England.) But just about every imaginable trick and strategy for bringing a drawing and page layout to life can be gleaned from a close look at them.

Caldecott loved to poke fun at grownups, as in this slapstick scene, which first appeared in Washington Irving's *Old Christmas* (1875) and was reprinted in *The Graphic* (1876).

Watercolor from *A Sketch-Book of R. Caldecott's* (1883), a delightful grab bag
of Caldecott graphics designed as a gift book for the artist's fans

Caldecott was the incomparable innovator in this regard. His picture books, like Eadweard Muybridge's stop-action photographs of animals and people in motion, were original expressions of a forward-looking time: the age of rapid rail travel, instantaneous telegraphic communication, and the quintessential modern art form—the motion picture. Had Caldecott lived a generation or two later, he might well have headed for Hollywood.

Beatrix Potter saw Caldecott as a "pioneer" of the art form of which she herself was a master and ranked him as "one of the greatest illustrators of all." Replying with strong feeling to an American librarian who had written to ask whether she and Caldecott had ever met—no, they had not, she was sorry to say—Potter went so far as to acknowledge her "jealous appreciation" of his work. All her life, she said, she had wished to draw as well as he did.

Among Caldecott's many American fans were the women who, starting around 1900, set up the very first children's rooms at public libraries and made it their mission to provide children with only the very best books. To these dedicated librarians, Caldecott's picture books represented an ideal of artistry for other illustrators to emulate. In 1937 the leading librarians felt the time had come to establish

an award honoring distinguished achievement by an American children's book illustrator. They named the new prize the Caldecott Medal and awarded it for the first time the following year.

Writing in 1946, on the one hundredth anniversary of his birth, the American novelist and critic Hilda Van Stockum said of Caldecott: "He is always aiming at the next picture; his very figures seem to be pointing to it; one cannot wait to turn the page and see what happens next." It was this same quality that so captivated Maurice Sendak: "The word *quicken*, I think, best suggests the genuine spirit of Caldecott's animation, the breathing of life, the surging swing into action that I consider an essential quality in pictures for children's books." Like Potter before him, Sendak would dedicate himself to fashioning art for children that equaled in energy, grace, and sheer magic the drawings of the man who had made horses gallop on the page, the man who invented the modern picture book and could not stop drawing:

RANDOLPH CALDECOTT.

RANDOLPH CALDECOTT TIMELINE

1846 Born, March 22, in Chester, England

1861 Starts work as a clerk at the Whitchurch and Ellesmere Bank, Whitchurch, England; sells his first drawing to the *Illustrated London News* (December 7)

1867 Moves to Manchester after accepting a clerkship at the Manchester and Salford Bank

1871 Publishes the first of many drawings in *London Society* (February issue)

1872 Moves to London, renting rooms at 46 Great Russell Street, across from the British Museum; first publishes his drawings in *Punch* (June 22) and *The Graphic* (Autumn); exhibits in group show at the Dudley Gallery, Egyptian Hall, London; visits continental Europe for the first time to make sketches for *The Harz Mountains: A Tour of the Toy Country*, a travel book about northern Germany by Henry Blackburn

1873 Studies sculpture with Jules Dalou; *The Harz Mountains*, the first book illustrated by Randolph Caldecott, is published; becomes "London artistic correspondent" for the New York–based evening newspaper *The Daily Graphic*, for which he attends the Vienna World Exposition

1874 Makes the first of many visits to France

1875 Illustrates the book that firmly establishes his reputation, *Old Christmas: From the Sketch Book of Washington Irving*

1877 Travels to both France and Italy and makes drawings for *Northern Italian Folk: Sketches of Town and Country Life* by Mrs. Comyns Carr, published the following year

1878 Publishes his first two picture books, *The House That Jack Built* and *The Diverting History of John Gilpin*; from then onward, two new picture books appear each fall, along with various compilations

1879 Moves to Wybournes, a country house in Kemsing, near Sevenoaks, Kent

1880 Marries Marian Harriet Brind (March 18) in Chelsfield, Kent

1882 Takes a twenty-one-year lease on a country house in Frensham, Surrey; purchases the brick row house at 24 Holland Street, London, near Holland Park

1885 With Marian Caldecott, departs Liverpool aboard the R.M.S. *Aurania* (October 31), bound for New York

1885 Arrives New York (November 9) and continues south by train with stopovers in Philadelphia, Washington, D.C., Richmond, Charleston, Savannah, and St. Augustine

1886 Dies, February 13, St. Augustine, Florida

1900 Memorial sculpture by Alfred Gilbert unveiled in Artists' Corner, St. Paul's Cathedral, London. The painted cast-aluminum sculpture depicts a Breton child clasping a portrait medallion

1938 First Caldecott Medal presented by the American Library Association to Dorothy P. Lathrop for *Animals of the Bible: A Picture Book*, text selected by Helen Dean Fish (Frederick A. Stokes)

1983 The Randolph Caldecott Society UK holds its inaugural meeting; the Randolph Caldecott Society of America founded

RANDOLPH CALDECOTT: HIS BOOKS
The Picture Books
(all printed by Edmund Evans and published in London by George Routledge & Sons)

1878

The Diverting History of John Gilpin, by William Cowper

The House That Jack Built

1879

The Babes in the Wood

An Elegy on the Death of a Mad Dog, by Oliver Goldsmith

1880

Sing a Song for Sixpence

The Three Jovial Huntsmen

1881

The Farmer's Boy

The Queen of Hearts

1882

Hey Diddle Diddle and Baby Bunting

The Milkmaid

1883

The Fox Jumps Over the Parson's Gate

A Frog He Would A-Wooing Go

1884

Come Lasses and Lads

*Ride a Cock Horse to Banbury Cross and A Farmer Went Trotting Upon
    His Grey Mare*

1885

An Elegy on the Glory of Her Sex, Mrs. Mary Blaize, by Oliver Goldsmith

The Great Panjandrum Himself

Starting in 1879, Caldecott's enterprising publisher issued compilations of his popular picture books bound together in various formats.

Other Selected Books Illustrated by Randolph Caldecott

1873

The Harz Mountains: A Tour of the Toy Country, by Henry Blackburn (London:
    Sampson Low, Marston, Low & Searle).

1875

Old Christmas: From the Sketch Book of Washington Irving, by Washington Irving
    (London: Macmillan).

1877

Bracebridge Hall, by Washington Irving (London: Macmillan).

1878

Northern Italian Folk: Sketches of Town and Country Life, by Mrs. Comyns Carr
    (London: Chatto and Windus).

1880

Breton Folk: An Artistic Tour in Brittany, by Henry Blackburn (London:
    Sampson Low, Marston, Searle & Rivington).

1881

Factory Folk During the Cotton Famine, by Edwin Waugh (Manchester:
    John Heywood).

1883

Jackanapes, by Juliana Horatia Ewing (London: Society for Promoting
    Christian Knowledge).

Some of Aesop's Fables with Modern Instances, translated by Alfred Caldecott
    (London: Macmillan).

The Vicar of Wakefield, by Oliver Goldsmith (London: Kegan Paul,
    Tench & Co.).

1884

Daddy Darwin's Dovecote: A Country Tale, by Juliana Horatia Ewing (London:
    Society for Promoting Christian Knowledge).

1885

Juliana H. Ewing and Her Books, by H. K. F. Gatty (London: Society for
    Promoting Christian Knowledge).

Lob Lie-by-the-Fire, or The Luck of Lingborough, by Juliana Horatia Ewing
    (London: Society for Promoting Christian Knowledge).

1886

Jack and the Beanstalk: English Hexameters, by Hallam Tennyson (London and
    New York: Macmillan).

The Owls in the Belfry: A Tale for Children, by A. Y. D. (London: Field & Tuer).

Special Editions

1883

Randolph Caldecott's Graphic Pictures (London and New York: Routledge).

1887

The Complete Collection of Randolph Caldecott's Pictures and Songs (London and
    New York: Routledge). All sixteen picture books bound together.

More Graphic Pictures (London and New York: Routledge).

1888

The Complete Collection of Randolph Caldecott's Contributions to The Graphic
    (London and New York: Routledge).

Gleanings from The Graphic *by Randolph Caldecott* (London and New York:
    Routledge).

Randolph Caldecott's Last Graphic Pictures (London and New York:
    Routledge).

1899

Lightning Sketches for The House That Jack Built, introduced by Aubyn
    Trevor-Battye (Westminster: *The Artist*).

SOURCE NOTES

7 "grand sheet of drawings": Blackburn, p. 115.

8 "retail hatter": 1851 census transcription details for Crook Street, Holy Trinity [Parish], Chester, Cheshire [Eng.]. National Archive Reference: RG number: HO107; piece 2172; folio 378; page 31.

8 "accountant of standing": *Catalogue* (1888), p. 5.

9 "studious in the popular sense": Blackburn, p. 2.

10 "off-time": Blackburn, p. 3.

14 "Cottonopolis": Wall text for the exhibition Cotton: Global Threads, Whitworth Gallery, Manchester University, February 11–May 13, 2012.

15 "Manchester goods": Wall text, Cotton: Global Threads.

19 "predestination": RC letter to John Numerley, dated March 26, 1867. National Art Library, Victoria and Albert Museum, MSL/1981/38/2.

19 "quill-driver": RC letter to John Harrison, dated June 23, 1864, reprinted in Hutchins, p. 196.

19 "He came like a ray": William Clough, in *Catalogue* (1888), p. 24.

20 "He made hundreds": Alfred Caldecott, in *Catalogue* (1888), p. 18.

21 "I was not [even] mentioned": RC letter to John Numerley, dated January 28, 1870. National Art Library, Victoria and Albert Museum, MSL/1981/38/8.

22 "I am so packed": RC letter to John Numerley, dated January 28, 1870. National Art Library, Victoria and Albert Museum, MSL/1981/38/8.

24 "Manchester to London": Notation in undated RC sketchbook. Department of Prints and Drawings, Victoria and Albert Museum, 91 A18.

27 "making a drawing": RC diary, quoted in Blackburn, p. 115. It is not known what became of the diary—a tantalizing mystery!

27 "Had storks out of cases": RC diary, quoted in Blackburn, p. 115.

30 "London artistic correspondent": Blackburn, p. 58.

34 Mr. Clemens: Paine, ch. XCI (unpaged, Project Gutenberg).

34 "very hearable": RC letter to William Baker Etches, dated October 22, 1873, reprinted in Hutchins, p. 62.

34 "Do you want": RC letter to William Baker Etches, dated January 1, 1874, reprinted in Hutchins, p. 65.

35 "I have now got a workshop": RC letter to unidentified Manchester friend, no date given, quoted in Blackburn, p. 97.

35 "Only . . . talk of matters": RC letter to unidentified Manchester friend, dated January 17, 1875, quoted in Blackburn, p. 118.

36 "The world": Blackburn, p. 110.

36 "Please say that my line": RC "private" letter to unidentified recipient, no date given, quoted in Blackburn, p. 154.

36 "I fear": RC letter to Frederick Green, dated February 3, 1883, reprinted in Hutchins, p. 170.

37 "I stick pretty close": RC letter to unidentified Manchester friend, dated January 17, 1875, quoted in Blackburn, p. 117.

38 "I feel I owe somebody": RC letter to unidentified recipient, dated April 27, 1875, quoted in Blackburn, p. 127.

45 "the land of cider": RC letter to William Clough, dated August 29, 1878, reprinted in Hutchins, p. 30.

45 "Sitting on Inn benches": RC letter to William Clough, dated August 29, 1878, reprinted in Hutchins, p. 30.

49 "A history of the twins was": RC letter to William Clough, dated October 1, 1878, reprinted in Hutchins, p. 32.

49 "any relation": RC letter to William Clough, dated December 13, 1878, reprinted in Hutchins, p. 33.

50 "catching . . . from the top": RC letter to Juliana Horatia Ewing, dated June 23, 1884, reprinted in Hutchins, p. 112.

51 "I scribbled out the plan": RC letter to William Clough, dated November 8, 1879, reprinted in Hutchins, p. 38.

53 "an out-of-way place": RC, quoted in Blackburn, p. 197.

53 "We were married": RC letter to an "invalid friend in Manchester," 1880, but no date given, quoted in Blackburn, p. 201.

54 "People . . . for whom I promised": RC letter to Frederick Green, dated September 9, 1883, reprinted in Hutchins, p. 173.

56 "We hope": RC letter to Frederick Locker-Lampson, dated November 18, 1885, reprinted in Hutchins, p. 245.

58 "organic disease of the heart": official death certification, dated February 13, 1886, and signed "H. Caruthers, Physician," quoted in Billington, p. 54.

59 "pioneer": Beatrix [Potter] Heelis letter to Jacqueline Overton, dated April 7, 1942, reprinted in Taylor, pp. 441–43.

60 "He is always aiming": Van Stockum, p. 120.

60 "The word *quicken*": Billington, p. 11.

BIBLIOGRAPHY

Alderson, Brian. *Sing a Song for Sixpence: The English Picture Book Tradition and Randolph Caldecott*. London, Cambridge, and New York: Cambridge UP in association with the British Library, 1986.

Archer, John H. G., editor. *Art and Architecture in Victorian Manchester*. Manchester, Eng.: Manchester UP, 1985.

Billington, Elizabeth T., editor. *The Randolph Caldecott Treasury*. Appreciation by Maurice Sendak. New York and London: Warne, 1978.

Blackburn, Henry. *Randolph Caldecott: His Early Art Career*. London: Sampson Low, Marston, Searle & Rivington, 1886.

Bodger, Joan H. "Caldecott Country." *The Horn Book* (June 1961): 227–38.

Brookman, Philip, Marta Braun, Andy Grundberg, et al. *Helios: Eadweard Muybridge in a Time of Change*. Washington, D.C.: Steidl/Corcoran Gallery of Art, 2010.

Catalogue of a Loan Collection of the Works of Randolph Caldecott Exhibited at the Brasenose Club. Manchester, Eng.: John Heywood, 1888.

Cech, John. "Remembering Caldecott: *The Three Jovial Huntsmen* and the Art of the Picture Book." *The Lion and the Unicorn* (1983–84): 110–19.

Crane, Walter. *An Artist's Reminiscences*. London: Macmillan, 1907.

Davis, Mary Gould. *Randolph Caldecott: An Appreciation*. New York and Philadelphia: J. B. Lippincott, 1946.

Doré's London. London: Chartwell, 2008.

Engen, Rodney K. *Randolph Caldecott: "Lord of the Nursery."* London: Bloomsbury, 1976.

_____. *Walter Crane as a Book Illustrator*. London: Academy Editions; New York: St. Martin's, 1975.

Finlay, Nancy, compiler. *Randolph Caldecott: A Checklist of the Caroline Miller Parker Collection in the Houghton Library*. Cambridge, Mass.: The Houghton Library, Harvard College Library, 1986.

Hutchins, Michael, editor. *Yours Pictorially: Illustrated Letters of Randolph Caldecott*. London and New York: Warne, 1976.

Keene, Derek, Arthur Burns, and Andrew Saint, editors. *St. Paul's: The Cathedral Church of London, 604–2004*. London and New Haven: Yale UP, 2004.

Marcus, Leonard S. "Medal Man: Randolph Caldecott and the Art of the Picture Book." *The Horn Book* (March/April 2001): 155–70.

McLean, Ruari, editor. *The Reminiscences of Edmund Evans*. London: Oxford UP, 1967.

Miller, Bertha Mahony. "Randolph Caldecott." *The Horn Book* (July 1938): 219–23.

Overton, Jacqueline. "Edmund Evans, Color-Printer Extraordinary." *The Horn Book* (March 1946): 109–18.

Paine, Albert Bigelow. *Mark Twain: A Biography, 1835–1910*. Project Gutenberg: http://www.gutenberg.org/files/2988/2988-h/2988-h .htm#2H_4_0058.

Parrish, Anne. "Flowers for a Birthday: Kate Greenaway, March 17, 1846." *The Horn Book* (March 1946): 97–108.

Randolph Caldecott, 1846–1886: A Christmas Exhibition of the Work of the Victorian Book Illustrator [held at] Manchester City Art Gallery. Manchester, Eng.: Manchester City Art Gallery, 1977.

Solnit, Rebecca. *River of Shadows: Eadweard Muybridge and the Technological Wild West*. New York: Viking, 2003.

Taylor, Judy, editor. *Beatrix Potter's Letters*. London and New York: Warne, 1990.

Van Stockum, Hilda. "Caldecott's Pictures in Motion." *The Horn Book* (March 1946): 119–25.

White, Jerry. *London in the 19th Century: A Human Awful Wonder of God*. London: Vintage, 2008.

Collections consulted include the British Museum, Department of Prints and Drawings; the Houghton Library, Harvard College Library, Caroline Miller Parker Collection; Leighton House Museum (London); the Manchester City Art Gallery, Manchester (Eng.); the Morgan Library and Museum, Literary and Historical Manuscripts; Museum of London; the National Gallery (London); the New York Public Library, Archives and Rare Books Division; the University of Minnesota Libraries, Kerlan Collection; the Victoria and Albert Museum, Department of Prints and Drawings and National Art Library; the Whitworth Art Gallery, University of Manchester, Manchester (Eng.); the Worcester City Art Gallery & Museum, Worcester (Eng.); and the private collections of Morton Schindel and Johanna Hurwitz.